INSTRUMENTAL PLAY-ALONG

MOVIE HITS

Alto Saxophone

Alto Saxophone

INSTRUMENTAL PLAY-ALONG

MOVIE HITS

SOLO ARRANGEMENTS OF 14 GREAT FILM SONGS WITH CD ACCOMPANIMENT

HOW TO USE THE CD ACCOMPANIMENT:
A melody cue appears on the right channel only.
If your CD player has a balance adjustment, you can adjust the volume of the melody by turning down the right channel.

HLE

HAL LEONARD EUROPE
DISTRIBUTED BY MUSIC SALES

Exclusive Distributors:
Music Sales Limited
14-15 Berners Street, London W1T 3LJ, UK.

Order No. HLE90002891
ISBN-13: 978-1-84609-373-9

Printed in the USA

Your Guarantee of Quality
As publishers, we strive to produce every book to the highest commercial standards. The book has been carefully designed to minimise awkward page turns and to make playing from it a real pleasure. Throughout, the printing and binding have been planned to ensure a sturdy, attractive publication which should give years of enjoyment. If your copy fails to meet our high standards, please inform us and we will gladly replace it.

www.musicsales.com

Contents

1 AN AMERICAN SYMPHONY

(Movement 3 Excerpts)

from MR. HOLLAND'S OPUS

ALTO SAX

By MICHAEL KAMEN

2 BACK TO THE FUTURE

from the Universal Motion Picture BACK TO THE FUTURE

ALTO SAX

By ALAN SILVESTRI

3 BELIEVE

from Warner Bros. Pictures' THE POLAR EXPRESS

ALTO SAX

Words and Music by GLEN BALLARD
and ALAN SILVESTRI

5 THEME FROM E.T. THE EXTRA-TERRESTRIAL

from the Universal Picture E.T. THE EXTRA-TERRESTRIAL

ALTO SAX

Music by
JOHN WILLIAMS

4 COME WHAT MAY

from the Motion Picture MOULIN ROUGE!

ALTO SAX

Words and Music by
DAVID BAERWALD

mp
mf
D.S. al Coda
CODA
f
mp
f
rall.
mf

6 FORREST GUMP – MAIN TITLE

(Feather Theme)

from the Paramount Motion Picture FORREST GUMP

ALTO SAX

Music by
ALAN SILVESTRI

❼ THEME FROM 'JURASSIC PARK'

from the Universal Motion Picture JURASSIC PARK

ALTO SAX

Composed by
JOHN WILLIAMS

8 LEARN TO BE LONELY

from THE PHANTOM OF THE OPERA

ALTO SAX

Music by ANDREW LLOYD WEBBER
Lyrics by CHARLES HART

❾ MISSION: IMPOSSIBLE THEME

from the Paramount Motion Picture MISSION: IMPOSSIBLE

ALTO SAX

By LALO SCHIFRIN

10 MY HEART WILL GO ON
(Love Theme From 'Titanic')

From the Paramount and Twentieth Century Fox Motion Picture TITANIC

ALTO SAX

Music by JAMES HORNER
Lyric by WILL JENNINGS

Irish Flute/Guitar
f
mp
rit.
p
Orch.

11 THEME FROM 'SCHINDLER'S LIST'

from the Universal Motion Picture SCHINDLER'S LIST

Composed by JOHN WILLIAMS

ALTO SAX

12 THEME FROM SPIDER-MAN

from SPIDER-MAN

ALTO SAX

Written by BOB HARRIS
and PAUL FRANCIS WEBSTER

13 STAR TREK® THE MOTION PICTURE

Theme from the Paramount Picture STAR TREK: THE MOTION PICTURE

ALTO SAX

Music by
JERRY GOLDSMITH

14 YOU MUST LOVE ME

From the Cinergi Motion Picture EVITA

ALTO SAX

Words by TIM RICE
Music by ANDREW LLOYD WEBBER